THE MOST Unusual Pet

Jeni Mawter

Illustrated by Paul Könye

Contents

ETA Cuisenaire

CHAPTER 1

All Kinds of Pets

Eric and Dad sat in the park.
They watched all the people walking their dogs.

Dad, can I have a dog?

No. Our backyard is too small.

Eric watched a bird fly onto the bench.

"We're not getting a pet," said Dad.
"I'm sorry, Eric, but that's final."

Eric and Dad went shopping that Saturday.
They walked past Hill's Pet Shop.
Eric stopped to look at the pets.
There was a big poster in the window.

Miss Hill saw them looking at the poster.

The pet show is next Saturday. Here's an entry form.

We won't need an entry form. We don't have any pets.

"Keep the entry form," said Miss Hill.
"Just in case you change your mind."
"Thanks," said Eric.
He took the entry form and put it in his pocket.

Six Days to Go

Eric and Dad started walking home.
They ran into Amanda.
Amanda was in Eric's class at school.

There's a pet show next Saturday.

I know.
I've entered my duck, Dixie.

Are there prizes for ducks?

No.
But there's a prize for the most unusual pet.

Eric thought about the pet show as they walked home.
There were prizes for dogs and cats.
There were prizes for birds and fish.
There were prizes for rabbits and mice
and guinea pigs.

Eric was sure he could win a prize.
But first he needed a pet!

Eric read the entry form when he got home.
There was a final date for entering.

CHAPTER 3

Eric Gets to Work

Eric was extra good for the next few days.

SUNDAY
He washed
the car.

MONDAY
He cleaned
his room.

TUESDAY
He washed
the dishes.

WEDNESDAY
He asked
if he could
have a pet.

Everyone else in Eric's class had entered the pet show.
That made Eric feel worse.
Eric knew they all had pets – and he didn't!

It was already Thursday.
The final date for entering was tomorrow.
How was Eric going to get a pet in time?

CHAPTER 4

A Surprise in the Toolbox

Eric got up early on Friday morning.
He went out to the garage.
He swept the floor.
He put all the tools where they belonged.
Then he cleaned all the tools in Dad's toolbox.

Dad came out to see what Eric was doing.

You've done a great job, Eric!
But I'm sorry, you still can't have a pet.

Eric was disappointed.
Dad would never let him have a pet!

Suddenly Dad looked in the toolbox.

"This is Frank," said Dad.
He pointed to a little black spider.

15

CHAPTER 5

Just in Time!

Eric asked Dad about the pet show.

Can I put Frank in the pet show? He could win the most unusual pet prize!

Well, he is a pet. And he is unusual. Is there still time to enter the show?

Yes!

That afternoon Eric made this sign.

FRANK
the Toolbox
SPIDER

Then Eric and Dad went to Hill's Pet Shop.
Eric gave the entry form to Miss Hill.

CHAPTER 6

At the Pet Show

The pet show was popular.
There were people and pets everywhere.
Eric and Dad carried the toolbox
to **The Most Unusual Pet** table.
They put it with the other entries.

19

It was soon time to give out the prizes
for The Most Unusual Pet.

Tim waved his lizard in the air.

Amanda had a great big grin on her face.
She ran up to get her ribbon.

"Congratulations," said Dad.
"Go and collect your prize."

Eric came back to Dad.
He wasn't holding a prize.

CHAPTER 7

The Mystery Prize

Eric and Dad stood near the monkey cage at the zoo.
They watched the monkeys climbing and jumping.
The zookeeper pointed
to a monkey.

See that monkey?
He's your prize.
The pet shop has given us money
to take care of him.
You can visit him
as often as you want.

The monkey came over to the fence.
It grinned at Eric.

I'm going
to call him Pal.
Now I've got
two very unusual pets—
Frank and Pal!